The Viking Explorers

Vikings Attack Paris

The Viking Explorers

Never in history was there a more venturesome breed of men than the Vikings of Scandinavia. In their small, swift ships they ranged the coasts of Europe, North Africa and even Asia, sailing far up rivers to pillage, trade and exact tribute from hundreds of thousands of people. Author Walter Buehr tells in this gripping account how they conquered the British Isles, colonized Iceland and Greenland — and then sailed on to become the discoverers of North America.

THE VIKING EXPLORERS

by Walter Buehr

G. P. Putnam's Sons   New York

Books by Walter Buehr

Through the Locks: Canals Today and Yesterday
Treasure: The Story of Money and Its Safeguarding
Harbors and Cargoes
Trucks and Trucking
Knights, Castles and Feudal Life
Railroads Today and Yesterday
The Crusaders
Sending the Word: The Story of Communications
The Genie and the Word: Electricity and Communication
Keeping Time
The Story of the Wheel
The World of Marco Polo
The French Explorers in America
The Spanish Armada
The Spanish Conquistadores in North America
Chivalry and the Mailed Knight
Westward — With American Explorers
Heraldry — The Story of Armorial Bearings
Famous Small Boat Voyages
Galleys and Galleons
The Portuguese Explorers
The Viking Explorers
Freight Trains in the Sky *948 Bue*

Fourth Impression

Published simultaneously in the Dominion of
Canada by Longmans Canada Limited, Toronto

Library of Congress Catalog Card Number: 67-24146
PRINTED IN THE UNITED STATES OF AMERICA
12216

Chapter I

The river flowed placidly down the quiet valley between wooded hills until its waters mingled with the cold gray waves of the North Sea. Its banks were silent and deserted. No smoke plumed above the trees, no cattle or sheep grazed among the lush meadows.

The Frankish peasants native to this land knew better than to build their huts near the river mouth where a pirate fleet might swoop in from the sinister sea at any moment. They always built well upstream to give time to close the log gates of their palisades and string their bows in time of peril.

No sound broke the silence on this summer morning early in the 9th Century except the lapping of the waves on the gravel shore and the shrill crying of gulls as the rising sun shone faintly through the morning mists along the horizon.

The peasant boy wrapped in a heavy woolen cloak stretched and yawned and got stiffly to his feet at his post on a hilltop overlooking the river mouth. His job was to watch for any strange craft approaching the river and warn the village of anything suspicious. But nothing had broken the great arch of the horizon since he had relieved another watcher two days ago, and he was getting bored with scanning the empty sea.

He reached into his greasy leather wallet for his breakfast of coarse black bread and cheese, but before he could take a bite, something far out in the swirling mist caught his eye. As he stared, his heart began to pound. Yes, there it was again, a dark shape low in the water, then another and another. Suddenly the sun caught the edges of sails and glinted from flashing oar blades. Now he could see the fierce dragon heads rising above the graceful hulls and the flashes of light reflected from polished helmets, spear points and sword blades.

The boy turned and fled, panic speeding his heels, to warn the village that the Vikings, those dreaded cruel raiders from the north, would soon be upon them. This flotilla of Viking sea raiders consisted of six ships, lightly built and shallow of draft, designed for speed and for operating in shallow water under sail and oars. Along each gunwale hung a line of brightly painted shields, one overlapping the next, two shields to each oar hole. Each dragon-ship was pro-

Viking Raiders Appear out of the Haze

pelled swiftly by 16 pairs of oars, 17 to 19 feet long. From a yard slung across the 40-foot pole mast hung the single red-and-white striped square sail.

The crews of the raiders, anywhere from 18 to 30 men, depending on the size of the ship, were tall, bearded and moustached Scandinavians. They wore mail shirts of interlaced steel rings which reached almost to the knees, over which were slung handsome, fur-trimmed cloaks, fastened at the throat by jeweled gold or silver brooches called *fibulae.* Loose trousers and leather shoes whose laces were crisscrossed around the trousers to the knees were visible below their cloaks. On their heads were conical steel helmets. Each man carried into battle a long, two-edged sword, a battle-ax, a spear and a short knife, as well as a round wooden shield with a metal boss.

The captain of each dragon-ship was also the steersman, who stood on the *lypting* — an elevated platform in the stern — gripping the thwart-ship steering tiller. This was fastened to the 11-foot steering oar or rudder, which was pivoted outboard, outside of the starboard quarter. From the lypting he could look down on his crew, direct their attack, and maneuver the ship.

The dragon-ships sped silently up the river, the only sound the slight splash of the oar blades as they cut the water, for surprise was one of the Norsemen's most effective weapons. At last the leading ship rounded a bend and sighted their goal, a small Frankish village

8

of huts built of mud-daubed wattled walls, surmounted by ragged roofs of thatch. A dirt wall topped by a stockade of pointed logs surrounded the village, but the log gate stood open, sheep and cattle grazed in the meadows behind the houses, and flocks of geese and ducks quacked along the river bank. The swift Viking ships had beaten the coast watcher with his warning!

Suddenly the village dogs set up a clamor of hysterical barking. Too late, the peasants discovered sinister dragon-headed ships being beached along the shore. Before they could flee behind the walls, the tall bearded strangers leaped from their ships with fierce cries and charged through the gate, swinging their great axes, slaughtering men, women and children, looting the houses and then setting them afire. Soon, save for a few villagers spared to become slaves, all were killed in the bloody massacre. The village was a heap of smoking embers.

The Vikings butchered some of the cattle and sheep and roasted them over cooking fires along the shore, washing down the great joints of meat with captured beer and some of their own mead — a drink made of fermented honey.

Next morning Viking warriors scattered through the countryside capturing as many horses as they could find. Then, leaving a third of the men behind to guard the boats, the others mounted and swept over the cart tracks along the river, overwhelming village after village, putting to death the inhabitants, and pillaging and burning the homes.

Several days later, the column, laden with silver, weapons, cloth and slaves, returned to their beached ships, loaded them with their loot, and headed downstream to disappear behind the haze on the horizon. They had vanished long before the Frankish king could assemble an army large enough to attack them.

For two hundred years the coasts of Europe, England, Scotland, Ireland, even North Africa and far-off Russia, trembled before the savage raids of the tall Northmen. No place which could be reached by the swift dragon-ships ever felt safe. It was true, however, that life a thousand years ago was brutal and merciless everywhere.

The Vikings were not especially more ruthless than the Scots, the Franks, the Arabs or the Irish, who behaved in the same way whenever they could. The Vikings were simply better warriors. Their swift dragon-ships, which gave them control of the sea, made it possible for them to run far up European rivers and fall upon inland towns with lightninglike, savage raids.

Who were these fierce Norsemen, who during 250 years in the 9th, 10th and 11th Centuries terrified all Europe with their sea-borne attacks? Later they occupied and settled Scotland, Ireland, Iceland, Greenland, much of England, Normandy and Russia, and traded as far to the east as Constantinople and Baghdad. They came from what is now Norway, Sweden and Denmark. There they had lived for hundreds of years, minding their own business and fighting only among themselves — until the beginning of the 9th Century.

By that time they had become the best boat-builders and seamen in the world. They had produced the famous long-ships which could cross long stretches of open water. By that time, too, the Scandinavian Peninsula and the Danish Islands were beginning to be overcrowded. Farmers were finding it harder in that cold bleak land to fill the hungry mouths of an ever-increasing population. Something had to give, and the year 787 or 789 A.D. marked the beginning of the Norse terror.

Not all Norsemen were fierce-raiding Vikings. Many were peaceful traders whose voyages covered almost the entire civilized world. True, some of these traders would occasionally attack peaceful natives, if they had the chance, and take prisoners whom they sold as slaves in the trading towns. The word "Vik," from which Viking is derived, has several meanings. One is a fjord, or bay. Another is a retiring place — thus a place from which the Vikings could pounce on their victims.

The Norsemen spoke of going "a-viking." By this they meant organizing an armed raiding party to attack some peaceful town, slaughter the inhabitants, and loot whatever they could carry away. Today the term "Viking" is often used to describe all the Norsemen of that great era.

The age of the Vikings dates three hundred years

before writing was known in Scandinavia. What archaeologists and historians know about the exploits of the Norsemen of the 9th, 10th and 11th Centuries had to be learned in roundabout ways. The tales of Norse heroes and their great deeds were kept alive in epic poems called *sagas*. These were composed by Norse poets and reciters, called *scalds*, who memorized and handed them down generation after generation, until at last scholars were able to write them. The time elapsed between an event and its recording naturally left many gaps and inaccuracies which may never be solved.

Another way of recording history was by runes, an ancient pictorial and alphabetical method used by the early Germanic and Scandinavian tribes. The characters were chiseled into flat stones, called rune-stones, to commemorate the death of a loved one or to record some important happening. Great numbers of these rune-stones have been found in widely scattered places and translated by modern archaeologists.

One of the richest fields for the scholars are the grave-mounds and boat graves of the pre-Christian Scandinavians, who until about the 10th Century worshiped their pagan gods — Odin, Thor, Frey and many others. They buried their dead in several different ways. Some were cremated, but others often placed the bodies, dressed in their finest costumes, with their weapons, valuables, tools, dogs, horses, food and drink

Carving a Rune-stone

— everything, they might need or desire in Valhalla, their heaven — in beautifully carved beds. Then the dead and their possessions either were cremated or buried under huge earth mounds. The custom ceased when the Norse became Christians because cremation and the burial of any objects with a corpse were forbidden by Church law.

Evidence from some early pagan graves of important men indicates that their favorite wives or slaves apparently were strangled and placed alongside the bier of the master. Usually they were placed in a wooden burial chamber so that they could serve him in the hereafter.

In Norway and Sweden, especially, corpses of chieftains were often placed in their own dragon-ships, surrounded by their arms, valuables, furniture and animals. Then ship and all were buried under huge mounds of earth. Archaeologists have been excavating these mounds for many years and have made rich finds of arms, implements, tools, fabrics, and entire longships with oars and masts. These findings vividly picture what life must have been like among the Vikings who lived a thousand years ago.

One of the most valuable discoveries was excavated at Gokstad in southern Norway in 1880. The mound, of blue clay, was 162 feet wide and 16 feet high. When the mud was cleared away, a Viking ship 76 feet long and 17½ feet wide, with a draft of 6½ feet from gunwale to keelson, was revealed, in very good condition. The mast had been cut off at the height of a timbered burial chamber built across the stern, which had long ago been broken into by thieves. The valuable objects of gold or silver had been removed, but part of a leather purse, an ax, a belt buckle and fragments of woolen cloth embroidered in gold remained.

On the deck were found 3 rowboats and 5 beds, a carved sleigh and the bones of 12 horses and 6 dogs, slaughtered to accompany their master to Valhalla. Amidships were found bronze and iron pots, cups, plates, candlesticks, barrels and wooden spades. On deck were found 16 pairs of oars, and in the bows an iron anchor, much rusted. Each gunwale of the Gokstad ship was lined with 32 round shields, each overlapping the next, painted alternately yellow and black.

The body of the highborn chief, whose grave this was, had been laid out on an intricately carved bed, wearing rich garments and surrounded by his arms. But the graverobbers had removed it from the burial chamber and pillaged the furnishings, leaving the skeleton of what had been a powerful middle-aged man of about six feet lying on the deck.

Students of Viking life had one other source of information — manuscripts written by scribes in lands where writing was known long before it reached the Norse. In the libraries of ancient monasteries and museums patient searchers have found accounts of Viking raids, of bloody battles and the conquest of entire kingdoms by the fierce warriors from the north. These sometimes report heavy indemnities of silver paid by the native populations to induce the Vikings to leave.

Naturally in such manuscripts the Vikings were described as cruel, bloodthirsty, merciless raiders who left behind them only ashes and ruin. The Viking sagas, on the other hand, speak of their seaborne warriors as brave, fearless, heroic men, sailing forth on glorious adventures and bringing back rich treasures. It was what all brave fighting men were doing throughout the world of that day.

Chapter II

Most pictures usually show the so-called dragon-ship as having an open broad-beamed shallow hull, with high, gracefully curving stem- and stern-posts topped by carved ferocious dragon-heads or scrolls; a row of shields hung over both gunwales, and a single mast on which was mounted a square sail. From 10 to 20 pairs of oars ran out through oar holes piercing the sides below the rails. These holes could be closed by shutters to prevent leakage when the ship was heeling sharply.

The dragon-ships were very fast war vessels which drew so little water that they could run far up shallow rivers. Because of their flat bottoms they could be hauled up on a beach or be carried across dry land on rollers. For coastal raiding strikes they were unexcelled, but they could not carry enough cargo for long trading trips and they were not good sea-boats. Their low sides caused them to ship a great deal of water in rough seas, so that constant bailing was required to keep them from swamping. The Vikings had not discovered how to make pumps, so the bilges had to be bailed by passing up buckets of water and dumping them over the sides. This was slow, exhausting work. Sometimes even the most desperate work failed to keep the boat from filling.

Rows of oars were hard to handle in rough seas, as the Greeks and Romans found when their galleys ventured out into the Atlantic from the calmer Mediterranean. Also, the extreme length of the dragon-ships was a serious drawback in steep waves.

The decorative shields had to be taken from the rails as soon as the ships left harbor. Otherwise, the first big cross-sea would have washed them away. And by Norse law the carved dragon-post must be removed from the prow before entering a harbor.

The dragon-ship was completely open, offering no shelter for men or supplies during a voyage across the cold northern seas where snow and icy sleet often fell upon the shivering crew. Thus the Vikings found that for long trading voyages they needed ships with higher sides, some shelter for crew and stores, and more sail power.

Among the earliest boats in Scandinavia were the *umiaks*, with frames of wood, covered with hides waterproofed with pitch. They dated from the Stone

Viking Trading Ship →

and Bronze Ages. Later boat builders learned how to construct hulls with wooden planking. By the 7th Century there were wooden boats 60 feet long, with raised bows and sterns, and with masts and sails. The sails of Norse ships were of homespun wool, which stretched when wet. So diagonal strips of leather, crossing each other to make a diamond pattern, were sewn to the cloth to strengthen it. The yard holding up the sail was lowered in harbor or on the beach and laid lengthwise above the hull to form the ridgepole of a tent to shelter crew and stores.

Such cargo ships were often built with a broad cutwater at bow and stern, connected underneath by a shallow keel which cut down drift. Their sides rose higher than did those of the dragon-ships. They rarely carried more than four to six oars to a side, since a cargo ship would not have enough room to carry a large crew. Later and larger versions of these ships, carrying bigger cargoes, were called *knorrs*. These were mainly the vessels the Vikings used during their trading voyages and explorations to the western Atlantic.

The general Viking name for every kind of ship was *skip*, but each type had its own class-name. Warships were the *Dreki* (dragon), the *Skeid, Snekja, Skuta, Buza, Karfi* or *Herskip*, also known as the *langskip* (long-ship), largest of the warships. The size of a vessel was reckoned by the number of rowers. The space from one oarsman's bench to the next was called a "room," so that a ship was said to have 20 or 34 rooms. Some of the largest of the long-ships were over 160 feet long and carried crews of 120 men.

The Vikings gave their long-ships dramatic and beautiful names, such as "Deer of the Surf," "Horse of the Gull's Track," "Lion of the Waves," and "Sea King's Sleigh." The ships were ornamented with decorative carving, picked out in gold, and the hulls were gaily painted in bright colors. The sails were striped in contrasting colors and often bore embroidered designs in gold, silver or brilliant colors.

Norse sagas describe almost incredibly large fleets of Viking ships setting out on a conquest. One such fleet was said to consist of 2,500 fighting ships, accompanied by another large fleet of *vistabyrding*, or supply ships.

The Norse ships remained supreme on the sea until the 12th and 13th Centuries. Then the *Hansa Cog* appeared on the scene, built and sailed by traders living along the Baltic and North Seas. They were roomier, higher-sided, and had cargo holds below deck, as well as stern castles. They were superior to the Norse knorrs, and they spelled the death of Norse dominance over the trade routes of Europe.

One might think that a ship rigged with just one big square sail could make headway only when the wind was blowing from directly astern. But the Viking ships could sail surprisingly close to the wind by the use of a long pole called the *beitass*. In order to point close into the wind the yard would be braced sharply at an angle instead of being at right angles with the direction of the hull.

The hulls of Viking ships were built quite differently from modern wooden hulls. In these, the planks are fastened rigidly to the ribs of the frame with long bronze screws. The Viking ships were *lapstraked*, or clinkerbuilt. That is, each plank of the topsides lapped over the edge of the plank below it. It was held by soft iron rivets driven through both planks and the seams were calked with tarred rope. The planks were not bolted to the ribs, but were lashed to them with tough roots or willow twigs through cleats. This made the hull elastic instead of rigid, since the planks could twist slightly, and so could better withstand the strain and pounding of rough seas.

The rudder of a Viking ship, shaped like a huge oar with a long blade, was not hinged to the stern-post as in later vessels. It was always slung outside over the starboard quarter and was known as the *steuer-board* or steer-board, from which comes our modern term "starboard."

Partway down, the rudder was pivoted through a block to the hull. At the top a tiller set at right angles to the rudder athwartship was worked by the steersman. In shoal water the rudder could be raised by pulling on a rope running through a hole near the bottom of the blade. When it was down, it acted as a center-board.

A copy of the Gokstad ship was sailed from Norway to the United States in 1893 for the Chicago World's Fair. Her Norwegian captain reported that her rudder was a work of genius, easily handled in even the roughest weather.

The mast of a Viking ship was stepped in a heavy block of oak, shaped like a flattened fish, and called the mast-fish. This was lashed to several of the ribs on the bottom of the hull. Rigging was simple. All of it was made of braided strips of walrus hide, considered the toughest and most durable rope. One of the most valuable products exported by the Icelanders and Greenlanders was walrus hide, which was used for rope-making. Rigging ran through hand-carved hard-wood blocks.

The Vikings had anchors much like those of the 18th Century, made of iron with wooden stocks, shackled to iron chains, and carried in the bows. The knorrs often carried wooden-drum windlasses, and usually one or two ship's boats with removable masts, overturned and lashed to the deck. Because Norse ships lay so low in the water, they had no scuppers (slits through the gunwales just above the deck from which water could drain away), so all the water which came over the rails ran down into a well in the bilges

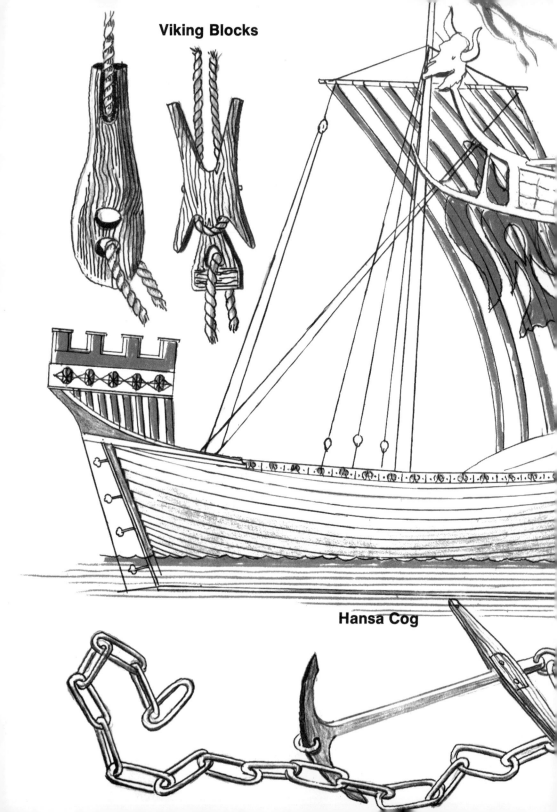

Viking Blocks

Hansa Cog

Early Norse Umiak

Viking Dragon Ship

from which it had to be bailed out laboriously.

Viking ships had no galleys. As a result, the crew had to eat cold food unless they could go ashore to build fires. Each crew member took his turn as cook. Knorrs had two unlighted crawl-spaces under the decks not more than 12 feet square and only 5 feet high in the center to house the crew of 15 or 20 besides the cargo. Passengers and slaves lived under tarpaulins on deck. Most crews slept in leather sleeping bags both afloat and ashore; on the beach they erected cloth shelter tents. In port they tied up close to the shore and put out gangplanks when they could.

Viking navigators carried only primitive navigating instruments. Nevertheless, they made long overseas voyages and managed to hit their targets again and again. This was long before the compass was invented and a thousand years before the chronometer. They navigated by observing the altitude of the stars above the horizon. By holding up a stick marked with a series of notches, called a *husanotra,* they could see how many notches above the horizon a certain star lay and so find their latitude. If they knew on what parallel of latitude their destination lay, they simply sailed north — or south — until they reached that parallel. Then they sailed along the parallel to their goal. It was the way Christopher Columbus and the navigators of his time sailed 500 years later.

The Vikings knew nothing of the 360 degrees or

the points of the compass or what north and south meant. They divided the circle of the horizon into eight segments which they called *airts*. Then they laid their courses by them, since they had neither charts nor compasses. Distance was reckoned in *doegr*. One kind of doegr was the distance a six-oared boat could be rowed during the daylight hours — about 30 miles. Another was calculated by the distance a boat could sail at about five knots in 24 hours — about 120 miles. Such measurements were, of course, inexact. The lengths of days were different during different seasons, and varying currents and winds would affect the distance sailed in a day. Thus the navigator had to average his speed during a voyage.

In the high northern latitude of Iceland, Greenland and Baffin Land there was no real sunrise or sunset during the summer by which a navigator could at least find east and west. In the far north the sun traveled erratically all around the horizon, dipping out of sight only for short periods. Since there was almost constant daylight during the summer, it was also difficult for the navigator to see the stars to take sights.

Chapter III

In battle a Viking's armor consisted of coats of mail called *brynjas*, made of interlocking steel rings. They had long sleeves and reached to a point somewhat above the knees. They looked something like the mail shirts of early medieval times. These brynjas were very expensive because they contained thousands of inter- locking welded steel rings and an armorer could only weld 200 to 250 rings during a long day. The Viking warrior had to pay 6 oxen or 12 cows for an iron breast- plate or helmet and 7 oxen for a sword.

It must have required many weary hours of patient rubbing to keep his armor, his sword and his battle-ax free from rust on a dragon-ship constantly doused with salt spray. Doubtless the warrior wore another coat over his armor to protect it as much as possible..

The Viking warrior carried a round wooden shield

faced with hide, on which was centered a metal boss with a knob or point. When he displayed a shield painted white to strangers, it denoted his peaceful intentions. A shield colored red meant battle.

Helmets were made in many designs. Some were leather caps reinforced by metal straps. Others were of interlaced strips of iron. Still others were decorated with pairs of bulls' horns or figures representing eagles, wild boars or other beasts admired for their courage.

The most important weapon of the Viking warrior was the sword on which he lavished much care and decoration. The pommels, grips and guards were often engraved with intricate designs into which gold, silver and copper and even precious stones were inset. The long, double-edged fine steel blades, three feet or more in length, were themselves often *damascened.* That is, gold or silver wire was hammered into grooves engraved into the steel, and then filed smooth, leaving a delicate golden design in the blade.

The early Norse swordsmiths were highly skilled. Many of their blades were made by welding strips of steel together into one blade. This made it tough enough to withstand mighty blows without breaking and still hold a sharp cutting edge. The Vikings also used the *sax,* a short curved single-edged sword with a broad blade.

Next in importance was the battle-ax, a mighty weapon in the hands of a Viking *berserker.* This man was an elite warrior who could work himself into such an insane rage during battle that he seemed to command the strength and fury of ten ordinary men. Often he would leap into the fray *"bare sark"* (without armor).

The Vikings used several types of spears, long-handled pole staffs, javelins, hewing spears and string spears, thrown for a considerable distance by a cord like a slingshot. Battle-axes with long handles were called *halberds*. The Norsemen used the six-foot longbow, but it was not their favorite weapon. They preferred personal combat.

Before they were converted to Christianity the Vikings worshiped many gods — Odin, Thor, Tyr, Baldr, Loki and many others. Odin was the god of warriors and battle. One reason the Vikings behaved so recklessly in battle and often seemed to welcome death was their belief that they would be borne in triumph by the Valkyries, the maidens who served Odin, to Asgard, the home of the gods. There stood Odin's vast hall, Valhalla, with 640 doors. Each slain warrior was enrolled in Odin's immense corps of immortals, the *einherjar*, and thereafter existed gloriously forever with the gods.

The Norsemen lived a harsh, active life in a land of long, cold winters. Mostly they were farmers, cattle- and sheep-herders, hunters and fishermen. They were particularly skillful boatmen, probably the best in the

world of their day. They lived in long houses, as much as 84 feet long, with curved sides, built either of logs, wattles (interlaced strips of wood daubed with clay) or turf, with walls sometimes 7 feet thick. The roofs were supported on rows of posts. The fireplace usually was in the center of the floor, without a chimney. A raised platform ran along each wall, on which the family sat or slept. Not until the Middle Ages did any sort of window appear. Thus the occupants sat in smoky darkness on the rush-strewn platforms with only the light of the fire and a torch or some primitive kind of grease-burning lamp.

Their kitchens were well supplied with pots and pans and kettles of iron or bronze, pottery bowls and jugs, ladles, spoons and knives. They had no forks.

They ate oats and barley porridge, rye bread, cabbage, onions, apples, berries, nuts and honey. Cheese, butter and cream were important additions to the menu, as were all kinds of fish, especially herring. For meat they slaughtered cattle, sheep and lambs, goats, horses, oxen and pigs of their own raising. When they could find them, they liked game birds, seals, bear and whale meat. Much of the meat and fish was dried, smoked or salted against a time of shortages and for sea voyages. They drank beer and mead. The wealthier drank wine traded from Frankish winegrowers.

They seemed to love fighting for its own sake and engaged in contests of arms for sport. The elaborate

A Viking Long House →

The Viking Sport of Stallion Fights

tournaments of medieval days, with mounted knights in full armor tilting against each other, were still far in the future. Still, there must have been contests with blunted long-swords, spear-throwing matches, and archery contests.

One popular spectator sport was the stallion fight, in which spirited horses fought each other fiercely with teeth and hooves. Sometimes the excitement reached such a pitch that the stallions' owners entered the fray themselves.

Falconry was very popular with the higher ranking Norsemen, as it was among nobles all over Europe at that time. The white Greenland falcon was considered the fiercest, fastest hunting hawk. Even the great kings of Europe were flattered to receive a Greenland falcon. So many nobles in Europe were eager to buy them that falcons became one of the leading exports of the 9th and 10th Centuries in Greenland. It gave the hard-pressed Greenlanders something to trade for badly needed ironware, grain and lumber. The Vikings also were fond of dice, and especially of chess. Many beautifully carved chess sets have been found in some of the earth mounds.

Chapter IV

It never has been clear just why the Norsemen who lived in the Scandinavian Peninsula and on the Danish Islands and Jutland suddenly erupted early in the 9th Century. They drove eastward deep into Europe, as far southeast as Constantinople and Baghdad, and south by way of the Mediterranean to Spain, North Africa and Italy. At the same time they crossed the North Sea, attacked England and Scotland, much of Ireland, and the French Channel coast. Presently they headed boldly out into the North Atlantic, settled Iceland and Greenland, and finally discovered the North American continent.

At the beginning of the 9th Century the Scandinavians had not yet become the kingdoms of Norway, Sweden and Denmark, each united under a king. They were divided into many fiefdoms, each under its own local king. Not only did the Norwegian chiefs fight against the Swedes and Danes, but all battled their own people. Princes deposed their royal fathers; uncles murdered royal nephews. Each local chief was ambitious and eager to raid and loot his neighbors.

By that time the Vikings had fine sea-boats and the skill to navigate them. They had picked up from foreign traders the knowledge that across the seas were lands filled with desirable goods they were unable to make for themselves. Since their warriors were fierce and well armed, why not give up the unprofitable and bloody wars among themselves and fare forth after easier and richer pickings?

About 787 A.D. the great Viking conquests began. In that year peasants plowing in the fields along the south coast of England noticed three strange ships with square sails, oars and high-curved stemposts surmounted by carved dragon-heads heading in toward the beach. Warning was sent to the soldiers, and a king's officer with some men galloped down to the beach, expecting to greet a company of merchants desiring to trade.

When the strangers landed, the officer, named Beaduheard, ordered them to come with him to the king's town for clearance. Instead, the tall strangers sprang upon him with their great two-edged swords and slew him and his men. This raid was soon followed by others. In June, 793, a small fleet of long-ships came ashore on the island of Lindisfarne, off the east coast between England and Scotland. Their Viking crews killed the devout Irish monks and looted the ancient monastery there. When they returned to their homes, probably on the west coast of Norway, they spread the word of easy conquest and rich booty across the sea. Soon dragon-ships filled with peasant warriors were swarming across the seas, eager for plunder.

During the next 200 years the Viking adventures took four different forms.

First came the quick raids by peasant chieftains on islands and coastal towns in England, Scotland, Ireland and the nearby coasts of Europe. They were hit-and-run attacks from which the Vikings returned at once to their home ports in Scandinavia.

Second came the larger, more formidable attacks along the coasts of the North Sea and the English Channel, usually launched in summer. In these the Vikings set up fortified camps, often on some island near the mouth of a river, which they could easily defend. There they organized raids in all directions, returning each time to their island base. Sometimes they even spent the winter in their camps and continued their attacks the next spring.

Third were the emigrating Vikings, crowded out of their homelands, who settled down in conquered territory, built homes, and finally cut off all ties with home. Sometimes they even fought on the side of the native inhabitants against new waves of Vikings trying to find a foothold in a new land.

Fourth were the later, peaceful Vikings of the mid-11th Century.

In the 9th Century the world was almost completely without roads. Except for Rome and Constantinople, the cities were only crude little towns with muddy alleys. In the countryside, except for the great Roman highways built centuries before, the roads were only rough, muddy cart tracks or trails.

Travelers and traders found overland trips slow, arduous and beset by brigands. So they often followed the coasts in small ships to the harbors nearest their destinations and then sailed or rowed up the great rivers to towns far inland.

These conditions were made to order for the Vikings in their swift, shallow-draft ships. The Swedes, whose land faced the Baltic, naturally turned toward the east. Their knorrs and long-ships traversed the Gulf of Finland and went up the Neva River to Lake Ladoga, thence by the Volkhov River to Novgorod, which became a Swedish trading port. From there, by following streams and sometimes portaging their vessels on rollers, they reached the mighty Dnieper and followed it southward to Kiev, which became another Swedish trading center. Continuing down the Dnieper to its mouth, they were swept into the Black Sea.

Once in the Black Sea they could sail up the Dniester into what is now South Russia, east of the Carpathian Mountains. If they chose, they could enter the delta of the Danube, which opened the kingdom of Hungary

and the Balkans to Viking traders. To the south they could enter the narrow straits leading to Constantinople, great capital of the Byzantine Empire, and the greatest city in the world.

Beyond Constantinople, by following the Sea of Marmara and the Dardanelles, they could enter the Aegean — beyond which all of the eastern Mediterranean lay open to them.

From the eastern end of the Black Sea it was not too difficult to reach the Tigris and the Euphrates and float down to Baghdad, the great trading center for the merchants from India and China. Traveling almost entirely by water, the Swedish traders were thus able to carry their slaves, furs, tallow, woolen cloth and iron-

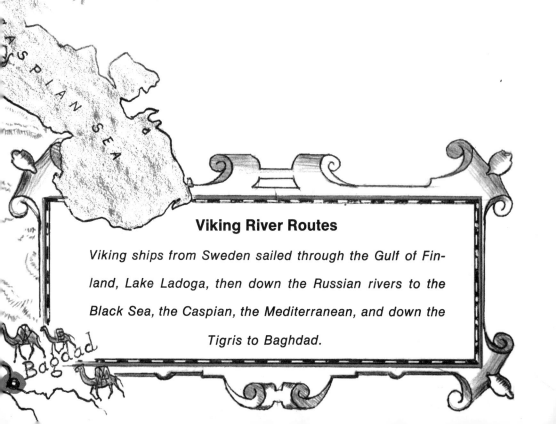

Viking River Routes

Viking ships from Sweden sailed through the Gulf of Finland, Lake Ladoga, then down the Russian rivers to the Black Sea, the Caspian, the Mediterranean, and down the Tigris to Baghdad.

ware into most of what is now Russia. There they traded with merchants from the East for silks, spices, glassware, gold and silver, precious stones, wine and oil. For hundreds of years this trade poured rich profits into Sweden.

The Danes, because of the location of their land, naturally steered their ships toward the southern coast of the Baltic — and up the rivers into what is now Germany and Poland. They also followed the North Sea coasts of present-day Holland, Belgium and France, passed through the English Channel and reached the Bay of Biscay. Both the Danes and the Norwegians raided the east and Channel coasts of England and the coast of the kingdom of the Franks (France). But Norwegian Vikings, whose coast faced westward toward the North Atlantic, made Scotland and Ireland, the Atlantic Islands, the Shetlands, the Orkneys, the Hebrides and the Faeroes their private preserves.

It was not long before the Norse reached Iceland, displacing the Irish monks they found living there. A hundred years later they pushed on to Greenland, which they found as yet uninhabited. The Norwegians' final thrust carried them to the coast of Baffin Land, Labrador, and — many historians believe — Newfoundland.

The great Swedish Viking drive to the east began in the 9th Century. By that time their dragon-ships and knorrs were crossing the Baltic, running up the Neva to Lake Ladoga, and then to the Volkhov and into other Russian rivers in great numbers. The Finns, the Slavs and other tribes encountered along the banks of the great rivers called the Viking invaders the "Rus." Many mounds have been uncovered along the shores of Lake Ladoga, proving that great numbers of Norsemen had passed that way.

One daring band of Swedish Vikings headed eastward in the year 859, a short time before Danish and Norwegian Vikings sailed westward in a great fleet to overrun England. The Swedes had heard tales from Christian and Jewish traders of a rich market town, called Novgorod, up the Volkhov River, which emptied into Lake Ladoga. It proved an easy capture with much rich plunder. Since they were not interested in settling down there, they demanded a huge ransom in silver from the citizens of Novgorod as a price for their departure.

This exploit came to the attention of a Swedish chief named Rurik, who assembled an army and fleet and landed on the Russian coast about the year 860. Rurik's men soon reconquered Novgorod, but he decided to stay for a while and trade with the native tribesmen who lived in the forests.

The natives were too distrustful of the piratical Vikings to meet them face to face to barter, as well they might, so they carried on "mute" trading. When a Viking trading party came to a bartering place not a soul was in sight. But the Norse placed some of their trading goods on the ground and departed. When they returned later, either they found their goods gone and a bundle of furs left in their place or they might see their goods still undisturbed. In that event they would add more goods to the pile until the natives were satisfied — or pick up their merchandise if they thought the natives too greedy. Eleven hundred years later Portuguese explorers reported the same kind of mute bargaining going on in Africa between the blacks and the Arabs for salt and gold.

For a while the Vikings, whom the natives here called Varangians, were satisfied to trade their furs, wax and honey for native products. But they soon found they could do much better by raiding the towns of the tribes inhabiting the river banks and demanding tribute from them. Presently Rurik and his Vikings were in complete control of all the territory from the Gulf of Finland down the Dnieper valley to Kiev.

As they pressed southward, the Vikings came to rapids and shoals which forced them to leave the ships that had brought them from Sweden. Then they transferred their possessions to smaller boats, many of them dugouts made by hollowing out huge logs. The upper reaches of the great Russian rivers — the Volkhov, the Volga, the Dnieper and the Don — are closely linked by small streams, though in some places dry land must be crossed. When the Vikings reached such portages, they cut logs or bundled brush to make rollers and simply pushed their dugouts to the next stream flowing in the direction they wanted to go.

Kiev, far down the Dnieper in what is now southern Russia, became one of the Vikings' main trading ports. The Byzantine Emperor Constantine Porphyrogenitus wrote in 950 a description of the trading operations of the Rus at Kiev.

He said that at the beginning of the winter all the Vikings headed by their chiefs left Kiev and went on a circuit into the lands of the Slavonic tribes who had been forced to pay tribute to them. They lived all winter in the deep forests among the Slav villagers, gathering furs from them as taxes. The richness and variety of fur-bearing animals in that land was almost beyond belief. Great bundles of black sable, beaver, sea otter, ermine, Siberian squirrel, fox and lynx were brought back to Kiev in the spring by the Vikings.

In Europe of the 8th and 9th Centuries furs were considered a badge of nobility. Only nobles were permitted to wear them and they were forbidden to the lower classes on pain of death. So the upper classes wore as many furs as they could afford, which assured a rich market for any the Vikings brought to Kiev.

The trip to the market town was fraught with hardship and danger. The way led through dangerous rapids where all the Rus disembarked, stripped naked, and waded, dragging their boats through the surging waters, dodging rocks and snags until they reached deeper water and could climb aboard again. Fierce local tribes living along the rapids attacked them, forcing the Rus to defend themselves while dragging their boats. After the ice had cleared to the north in the late spring, the Vikings made the long trip up river to the Baltic and across to their home ports in Sweden with their furs and goods.

Some of these "Rus" Vikings decided it would be easier to continue down the Dnieper to the Black Sea than to make that wearisome trip against the current to the north. Across the Black Sea lay Constantinople, the golden city, rich with the treasures Emperor Constantine had transferred from Rome when he moved his capital. Such a prize was too tempting to pass up. When Rurik's red-painted ships reached the mouth of the Dnieper in a fleet of 200, they sailed across the Black Sea to attack the Byzantine capital itself.

They might have succeeded since the emperor, Michael III, was absent with his fleet, fighting the Saracens in the Mediterranean. But a sudden storm capsized or wrecked most of the Viking ships and dispersed the fleet.

The disaster did not discourage the Vikings. They would try again because this great city was a tempting source of rich profits. At Constantinople the Norsemen could meet and trade with Arabs bringing caravans of goods from Baghdad, gateway of the East. Camels

46

laden with bolts of beautiful silks woven in China, gold, silver and jewels from India, spices from the Celebes — there were luxuries craved by both Scandinavians and other Europeans. Afterward they could return to Sweden by sea, by way of the Mediterranean, the Bay of Biscay, the Channel and the North Sea.

The Vikings soon discovered a kind of merchandise much desired by the Arabs throughout the East and in North Africa — slaves. In those times slavery was a normal state all over the world. Both the soldiers and the civilian populations of conquered lands who were not butchered immediately were enslaved by their conquerors. People guilty of certain crimes or those who could not pay their debts were enslaved, even by their own countrymen. Natives of foreign lands were rounded up by raiding parties and taken in chains to some slave market for sale. All children of slaves belonged to their masters and could be sold.

Native Norse slaves, called thralls, were already common in Scandinavia and imported ones were eagerly sought. So many Viking men had been killed in battle or were away on raids or voyages of conquest that there was a serious shortage of manpower to work the farms and go fishing.

For a long time, however, the Christian Church had been fighting slavery. Finally the king of the Franks had decreed that slaves could no longer be transported from Christian lands to Muhammadan countries. After that, any slaves the Vikings could deliver to Arab slave traders brought extra high prices. Such slaves ended up in the seraglios of Arab caliphs or as servants or laborers.

The vast wealth of Constantinople, with its beautiful churches and shrines filled with priceless vessels and holy objects of gold and jewels, drove Oleg, a Viking chieftain who succeeded Rurik, to attack the Byzantine capital again. With 80,000 men in a fleet of 2,000 ships, plus a large force of cavalry ashore, he advanced on the

city when the emperor's fleet again was away fighting the Moors.

The Vikings seemed so formidable that the emperor called a truce and offered them a large sum of money and a good trading agreement. In return they must always enter the city unarmed and only in small groups. The Vikings agreed.

Byzantine Ships Attack the Vikings with Greek Fire

For a time there was peace. Then another Viking chief named Igor, who succeeded Oleg, sailed out of the Dnieper with a huge fleet. Again he attacked the city while the imperial fleet was away. The defenders had only 15 leaky old vessels to match the great Viking fleet, but the Byzantine admiral fitted them out with tubes which could spew forth an inflammable liquid called Greek fire. His fire ships sailed out and poured such destruction upon the astonished Vikings that they fled in disorder while many of their ships burned to the water's edge. Later they took their revenge by attacking the countryside beyond the walls of the city, burning, murdering and looting.

While they were busy at their bloody task the Byzantine fleet of great triremes — which were much larger than the Viking ships — returned from the Mediterranean. They attacked and scattered the Norsemen, but Igor escaped and returned to the Dnieper where he raised an even larger army. This time ambassadors from the emperor met him before he reached the Bosporus and offered him rich gifts and a renewal of the trading treaty in return for peace.

After peace was declared the Byzantine emperor decided to recruit his personal palace guard from the tall, strong Viking warriors from Kiev, whom he admired. Not only were they fierce, able soldiers, but because they were men from a completely different background he hoped they would not plot against him.

A Viking noble named Harold Hardrada, who had

fled to Kiev from Norway as a boy of fifteen, was made commander of the Varangian (Viking) palace guard at Constantinople. He carried out successful attacks on four cities in Sicily and later led a campaign in Persia where he captured eight Arab cities for the emperor. His share of the booty made him wealthy.

In 1042 he returned to Norway where his nephew, Magnus the Good, had become king. Harold felt his claim to the throne was as good as Magnus'. The two finally entered into a friendly agreement whereby Harold would share his wealth with Magnus and Magnus share his throne with Harold. Soon afterward Magnus died and Harold ruled Norway alone for many years.

The Viking traders had always done business by bartering — furs for spices, slaves for bolts of silk. When they began dealing with the Arabs from Baghdad, however, they found a new and more convenient way of trading. The Arabs carried bags of silver coins to pay for what they wanted instead of bartering goods. As a result, the Vikings began hoarding these Arab coins to bring back to Sweden. A returned warrior might bury a cache of coins near his home for safekeeping and then meet his death in battle, leaving his hoard undiscovered. Thousands of these Arabic silver coins from many different caliphate mints, silver arm bands, rings, bracelets and necklaces have been unearthed in Scandinavia, England, Gotland and along the Baltic shores where their Viking owners had buried them.

Chapter V

During the 9th Century there were no great European nations with strong central governments. After the Roman Empire fell, the British Isles, Scotland, Ireland, Scandinavia, Germany, Italy and Spain were a complex of tiny kingdoms, dukedoms and earldoms. Each fought constantly with those around it; each had its own small, poorly trained army. Only in the land of the Franks — the France of today — was there a strong government under the Emperor Charlemagne. In that part of Spain that had been conquered by the Moors from Africa there also was rule by strong Arab caliphs.

These small bickering fiefdoms throughout Europe explain why a few thousand Vikings could attack and conquer lands where they were outnumbered a thousand to one. They concentrated their forces of fierce, well-trained warriors in lightning raids one at a time on small dukedoms which could get no help from jealous neighbors.

The Danes and some of the Norwegians struck along the North Sea and the Channel coasts of present-day Holland, Belgium and France and the entire east coast of England. Running up the rivers as far inland as their shallow-draft swift dragon-ships could navigate, they ravaged the towns. At first the raiders avoided the Frankish shores because Charlemagne had fortified his coast and harbors and kept warships and troops on guard. The Vikings always avoided heavy fighting if they could, preferring to loot unprotected towns. After Charlemagne died, his son, Louis the Pious, continued to keep a watchful eye on his coasts.

Godfred, the Danish Viking king, had a healthy respect for the great king of the Franks, whose borders lay just south of Denmark. After he had looted the Baltic Frankish town of Reric, he ordered a great wall to be built across the peninsula of Jutland to defend his lands from Frankish reprisals. The wall was made of earth, surmounted by a wooden palisade, in some places 18 feet high and 95 feet wide. About seven miles in length, it stretched from the fortified town of Hedeby on the Baltic side of the peninsula across to marshes on the North Sea. Besides protecting Denmark from the Franks it also protected a new trade route across the peninsula. Along this trade route Danish ships could reach the North Sea without passing through the dangerously narrow Kattegat around the tip of Jutland. Parts of this wall still may be seen, though it was built over a thousand years ago.

During the reign of Louis the Pious, while the two countries were on friendly terms, King Harold of Denmark and his retinue sailed peacefully up the Rhine River to Mainz. There he was baptized by Louis and returned to Denmark to spread the first seeds of Christianity among the pagan Scandinavians.

By the year 840 the Frankish Empire had become weakened by quarrels between the emperor and his sons. Harbor forts and coast defenses were neglected, the Vikings observed. As a result, Norse fleets under Ragnar Lodbrok sailed up the Loire in 843 and sacked and burned Nantes.

Ragnar was one of the greatest 9th-Century Viking warriors. His name "Lodbrok," according to legend, meant "hairy breeches." The name was a result of a feat he performed to gain his bride Thora, who was imprisoned in a castle surrounded by a moat filled with poisonous vipers. Ragnar made himself a pair of breeches of hairy goatskins, coated them with tar, and waded safely through the snake-filled moat to rescue his bride.

The Vikings grew steadily more daring. After a raid, instead of returning to Denmark, they often settled in a foreign country and laid waste the countryside around their base. Columns of smoke rose from burning vil-

lages along every river in France. The Franks grew increasingly despairing as they saw their loved ones slain, their property looted, and their homes burned.

Finally, in desperation, the Frankish king began to pay the marauders large sums of silver to make them leave. But the Vikings kept returning and demanding higher and higher payments.

In 859 the Vikings harried the west coast of France, looting Bordeaux and Toulouse. Finally they crossed the Bay of Biscay and reached Spain with 62 ships. There they encountered an unpleasant surprise. The Moors who had come from Africa and conquered most of Spain were well-trained, determined fighters who repulsed the Vikings decisively.

The Vikings then steered their dragon-ships through the Straits of Gibraltar into the Mediterranean. They harried the Moorish ports along the North African coast, attacked Sicily and the west coast of Italy, and drove east as far as Alexandria, Egypt. After these raids black slaves are mentioned in the Norse sagas as being sold in Scandinavia for the first time.

In 885 a huge force of Vikings sailed up the Seine in a fleet of 700 large dragon-ships filled with 40,000 fierce warriors led by a chief named Siegfried. They were heading for the wealthy province of Burgundy, but Paris, the city built on an island in the river, connected to each bank by stone bridges, barred the Viking ships.

Bishop Jocelyn, commander of Paris, refused the offer of the Vikings to spare the city if they were allowed to pass. So they attacked a tower guarding one of the bridges across the Seine. Twice repulsed, they retired to build huge rock-throwing machines and enormous triple rams to batter down the city walls. Assault after assault was hurled against the island fortress, but the walls remained unbreached throughout the winter and spring.

In August the Vikings attacked again. But King Charles, returning from a campaign in Italy with a large army, drove them off. Later, however, he allowed them to pass up the river to Burgundy and offered them a bribe of silver to leave France for good the next spring.

In the spring of 889 they returned. The Parisians refused to pay the bribe offered by King Charles and they drove the Vikings away. After that they never again threatened the city.

For 20 years after the Parisians drove out the Vikings, no Norsemen harried northern France. Then, in 911, a new Viking chief named Rollo, or Rolf, sailed into the mouth of the Seine with a strong fleet and army and built a fortified camp there.

At the time the Frankish king was Charles the Simple, who was not too simple to realize that he was not strong enough to drive Rollo away. He also knew that paying him a heavy tribute of silver would only lead to

Vikings Attack Paris

demands for more. The king therefore offered to give Rollo the land between the lower Seine and Brittany as his own if Rollo would agree to become a Christian and a loyal subject of the king, protecting his lands against raids by other Norsemen.

When Rollo agreed, he became the first Duke of Normandy. He and his men became Christians and adopted the manners, customs and clothes of the Franks. The duke and his descendants kept their promise to protect the king against both warlike Vikings from overseas and from his own rebellious dukes.

It was from this province of Normandy that Duke William, a descendant of the Vikings, led an army of Norman ex-Vikings across the Channel, defeated the English under Harold in 1066, and conquered England.

After the first Viking raids on the coasts of England late in the 8th Century, the Norsemen fell upon Ireland. For 20 years they looted and burned monasteries and villages and carried the people into slavery.

Then their hit-and-run methods changed. In 839 a chieftain named Turgeis landed with an army to remain and rule. By 840 he ruled all of northern Ireland. Following him came Olaf the White, a Norwegian, who won the title of King of the Northmen and of all Ireland and Britain. He ruled for 18 years.

During the 10th Century new waves of Viking invaders landed on Irish shores to battle both the native Irish and earlier Viking victors who now occupied the towns. In 1012 a great battle was fought between the

Irish under their new high king, Brian Boru, and his Viking allies, numbering 20,000 men, and the invaders. Brian Boru defeated them so roundly that few reached their ships. At last the Viking raids on Ireland were broken.

England itself was constantly being attacked and plundered. Canterbury and London were pillaged. York and East Anglia were occupied by Viking armies during the "Great Invasion" of 865, and then the Viking marauders spread out over the plains of England. No one could stop them until the Battle of Ashdown when the English King Aethelred and his son, who would be known as Alfred the Great, gave them a sound drubbing. When Alfred became king, however, the Vikings still were so powerful that he had to pay them tribute in silver.

Meanwhile, the Viking leaders who had landed in eastern England were distributing the land once owned by Englishmen to their Norse followers. Their idea was to settle permanently under their own laws and customs. From their strongholds they sallied out to raid — unless bribed.

King Alfred fought the Vikings steadily for years and managed to raise an army large enough to defeat the last great Viking attack of his reign in 892. At that time he met an 8,000-man army which had arrived from its unsuccessful siege of Paris, together with an army led by another chief, Hastings.

Alfred's victory made it possible for his son Edward,

who became king in 899, to drive out the Vikings and send them fleeing into the north of England. In the early 11th Century, however there were further Viking invasions. Finally the Danish King Sweyn Forkbeard conquered all of England, forcing the English king to flee to Normandy. After Sweyn's death, his son Canute was proclaimed king of all England, as well as of Denmark, Norway and Scotland.

Canute ruled wisely, allowing no Viking raids during his reign. Only one more great Viking invasion reached England after his death in 1035, near York, but it was defeated by an army under Harold of England. Before Harold's tired, battered troops could rest and refit, a greater disaster engulfed them. William of Normandy, the French descendant of Vikings, landed and overwhelmed Harold at the famous battle of Hastings. The Norman conquest put an end to the Vikings in England.

In the 11th Century the fierceness of Viking attacks began to slacken. Christian nations that once had lain helpless before their raids now grew strong enough to drive the Vikings from their coasts with heavy losses. The pagan invaders who had occupied Russia, France and England became Christians. Their loyalties lay more with their adopted homes than with the Norselands.

In the 9th Century a Viking had ventured north and eastward from Norway. His name was Ottar, a rich and powerful chief who lived in northern Norway. During his travels he encountered King Alfred of England, to whom he related his adventures during a long voyage around the North Cape, the northern tip of Norway. He spoke of his reindeer herds, of walrus teeth for ivory, of bearskins and birds' feathers which he had exacted from the Finns and Lapps as tribute. And he told King Alfred how other Vikings had discovered Spitzbergen which was so far north in the Arctic Ocean that it was encased in ice for two-thirds of the year.

North of Spitzbergen the Vikings feared to voyage. They believed that beyond lay the edge of the world, encircled by a fabulous serpent. But they did follow the coast of the White Sea eastward to discover Novaya Zemlya, an island which they found even colder than Spitzbergen. These lands east of the North Cape offered little encouragement for settlements.

By the 11th Century only one direction lay open to the Vikings — the west, across the gray, stormy Atlantic.

Viking Village in the Shetland Islands

Chapter VI

The Vikings explored westward step by step, sometimes purposefully, sometimes by being blown helplessly off course by storms.

Their first westward step was to reach the Shetland, Orkney and Faeroes Islands. These tiny dots in the rolling Atlantic are believed to have been inhabited first by seafaring Irish monks. But early in the 8th Century the monks, weary with repeated Viking raids, abandoned them to the Norsemen who homesteaded there.

One account states that in the middle of the 9th Century Nedd-Odd, a Viking who had been visiting the Faeroes, set out for home in Norway. But his ship encountered such violent easterly storms that the crew had to take in sail and bail for their lives for days. When the gale at last subsided and the weather cleared,

Nedd-Odd was surprised to sight a coast lined by high, forbidding, snow-clad peaks. He landed and climbed one of the peaks, from which he could see endless miles of mountains and glaciers. "Snow-land" was the name he gave this new land after the wind let him sail home to Norway.

Later a Swede named Gardar, who was also blown off course, discovered the same land and was forced to spend the winter there. On his return he bragged about *his* discovery which *he* called Gardarsholm, in his own honor. Hearing of the new land, a venturesome Norwegian named Floki Valgerdsson fitted out a small expedition of three ships and headed west to look for it. He sailed by way of the Shetlands and Faeroes, convenient stepping-stones along his course.

Floki, determining that the new land was an island, spent two winters there and gave it the name which stuck — Iceland. He found many birds and good fishing. But the cattle he brought with him died from lack of fodder and he had no desire to settle in Iceland.

Floki was followed by other emigrants, mostly from western Norway. They left their homes because they felt oppressed by King Harold Fairhair, who had united Norway by stern measures. These migrants bypassed the outer islands, which already had too many settlers and were plagued by constant pirate raids. When they arrived in Iceland they found they were not the first settlers. The great Irish saint, Brendan, had

Viking Helmet and Swords

Viking High Seat

led a colony of Irish monks across the sea in an open boat and left them in Iceland while he continued his wanderings. (Some believe Brendan may have reached the West Indies, which would have made him the discoverer of America.)

In any event, the first Viking settlers of Iceland told of finding Christian men already living there who left because they refused to live among heathen Norsemen. The Christians left behind croziers and bells and Irish books — curious objects to the Vikings, who did not yet have a written language.

The first settlers to stay in the bleak new land were Ingolf Arnarson and Leif Fyrdafylke. They brought their families and livestock.

In the home of every Norse chieftain was his personal seat of honor, flanked by two beautifully carved posts, called high-seat pillars. He took them with him when he sought a new home. When he sailed into a harbor where he planned to settle, he tossed the high-seat pillars overboard to float where the waves took them. Then he searched until he found where they had stranded ashore. On that site he built his house.

Ingolf Arnarson couldn't find his pillars for three years in Iceland, according to legend. When at last he did, at a place where a hot water geyser sent up clouds of steam, he built his house. He named it Reykjavik, meaning "warm springs." Today it is the capital of Iceland.

Geysers in Iceland

The Vikings found Iceland a strange island, a place of violent contrasts. The south and west coasts had a surprisingly mild climate, warmed by the gulf stream, with many hot springs and steaming geysers and good pasturage where the Norsemen could raise cattle and sheep and some crops. On the east coast, chilled by the polar currents, were tremendous glaciers which never melted, where the wind howled ceaselessly and only polar bears and walrus could exist. In other parts of the island the Norsemen were awed by roarings heard deep in the earth and by sudden fiery eruptions which cast glowing lava high into the air. Iceland, near the Arctic Circle, is one of the most active volcanic areas of the world.

Year after year, more Vikings came to Iceland and built turf-walled windowless huts, planted sparse crops, and tried to keep cattle, pigs and sheep alive through the long winters. Within 50 years there were more than 16,000 people on the island and the best land had been occupied. Thereafter newcomers had to buy land from earlier settlers.

The newcomers had abandoned the low, unseaworthy long-ship for the knorr. It was longer, wider, had higher sides, enclosed cabins, and shelter below decks. One might suppose the Vikings, in such seaworthy vessels, would soon have ventured farther westward. Yet it took them another century to reach Greenland, less than 200 miles to the west.

At last, late in the 9th Century, a Viking named Gunnbjorn, on his way to Iceland, was driven to the west by a gale and sighted a group of tiny islands off an icy mountainous coast. He named the area Gunnbjorn's Skerries. Nobody seemed much interested in his story of new lands when he returned to Iceland. It was almost a century later, in 982, before the unknown territory to the west was explored.

The explorer was a hot-blooded brawler named Eric the Red, who had been convicted of murder and sentenced to banishment from Iceland for three years — then the customary punishment for such a crime. Eric the Red and his crew headed westward to the bleak ice-bound east coast of Greenland. It was so forbidding that he made no attempt to land, but sailed south until he reached present-day Cape Farewell. Rounding it, he found himself among the deep fjords of the more friendly west coast. He named the area Osterbygden, or "eastern settlement."

Farther up the west coast, to the northwest, he landed in another promising area he called Vestbygden, or "western settlement." In the shelter of the mountains, protected from the Arctic north winds, he found good sites along the deep fjords where crops could be grown and livestock pastured.

Eric and his crew lived among these fjords during the three years of his banishment. They built huts with stone walls and thick turf roofs, hunted for seal, bear, walrus and narwhal, caught birds and fished for salmon and cod. The men built their fires of driftwood, for there were no trees on this new island. Later they learned to their sorrow that there was no iron ore either.

When Eric returned to Iceland he told all who would listen of the bountiful new land, with plenty of good pasturage and wonderful hunting and fishing. He was

Vikings Hunt the Walrus

so eager to encourage emigration that he even named his bleak, treeless island with its forever frozen glacial center Greenland!

His enthusiasm infected many Icelanders who lacked good farms. In the spring of 986 from 500 to 700 emigrants set sail in 25 ships, with their household goods, livestock, plows, seed and lumber for building. Only 14 of the ships arrived. The others either turned back or foundered.

When they reached Osterbygden, Eric picked the choicest land, on which he built Brattalid, his home-

stead, and proclaimed himself chief of Greenland. The remainder of the useable land was divided among the other immigrants.

Within 10 years 200 farms were built at Osterbygden and 100 at Vesterbygden. The hardy Vikings began a struggle to wrest a living from the harsh land which was to last more than 400 years. Ice and snow isolated them from October to May. During the short summer they tried to grow some grain and other crops, but without much success. They had to depend on fish and game and on their own sheep, cattle, goats and swine. From the cows' and goats' milk they made skyr, salted butter, and cheeses. They were good fishermen and hunters. The seals, bears, walruses, reindeer, and whales they killed supplied meat, clothing, footwear, weapons, and tools.

Since there was no lumber or iron on Greenland they had to barter for them with Icelandic and Norse traders. Furs, dried fish, walrus tusks and a high-quality cloth woven from the wool of their sheep were their exports. They also had two rather astonishing products to trade, which allowed them a few luxuries such as honey and wine. One was the long, twisted horn of the narwhal, an animal somewhat resembling a seal. Its long single hollow horn, twisted in a right-hand spiral, sometimes grew to nine feet in length. In those days the narwhal horn was believed to be from the fabled unicorn; it was greatly prized by doctors, who

Greenland Vikings Hunt Narwhals

ground it up to make medicines which were thought to have magic powers.

The other valuable export was the Greenland falcon. At European courts the hunting hawk valued above all others was the Greenland falcon, which the Vikings trained and exported at great profit.

Eventually 16 churches, 2 cloisters and a bishop's palace were built in the Greenland settlements. In 1327 the Christian Greenlanders sent the Pope's representative 250 walrus tusks as a tithe. Yet in the middle of the 16th Century a Norwegian expedition sent to investigate conditions in Greenland found not a single Viking alive.

There were several reasons for the disappearance of the colony. When the Vikings arrived, they found a completely uninhabited land. But Icelandic history of the late 13th Century records that by that time Eskimos, or Skraelings as they were called, were frequently seen in Greenland. During the 14th Century the kayaks of the great migration of Eskimos from Alaska were driving the Norsemen southward from their customary walrus hunting grounds. With no more ivory to barter, the Vikings no longer could obtain desperately needed grain, iron and lumber.

An even more vital reason which sealed their fate was the climate. The Vikings arrived in Greenland during one of the great warming swings of the climate. But later another cold era crept down from the Arctic.

The summers grew shorter and cooler, until the crops the Norsemen planted no longer ripened and pasturage for their stock was killed by frost. Norse skeletons of this period show they had rickets, twisted spines, dwarflike bodies — all signs of continual starvation. Proof of the climate change is shown by the fact that earlier Viking graves in Greenland were dug at least six feet deep, while those of the last inhabitants were barely deep enough to cover the coffins. By that time the ground never thawed more than a few inches during the summer.

Chapter VII

Almost five centuries before Christopher Columbus discovered America, Vikings landed on the North American continent. Precisely where they landed still is a subject of dispute among scholars. Indeed, it is not certain whether their "discovery" was by accident or design.

Two ancient sagas are the authorities for what we know of Viking voyaging beyond Greenland. Until comparatively recent times the *Flatey Book* formed the basis of knowledge about Viking explorations in what they called "Vinland." The *Flatey Book* abounds in contradictions, however. Another source, the *Saga of Eric the Red,* is favored by many scholars since it is supported by a number of other references in early Icelandic and other literature.

The *Saga of Eric the Red* tells this simple tale: In

999 Leif Ericsson, son of Eric, traveled to the court of King Olaf Tryggvason of Norway. There King Olaf commissioned him to spread Christianity in Greenland.

Leif, returning, was driven far off course to lands in America "of which he had previously had no knowledge" and which he called Vinland because of the wild grapes he found growing there. He also found wild wheat and "mosür" wood which he took back to Greenland with him. The description he gave of the country makes it sound much like present-day southern Nova Scotia. But here arises the first of many contradictions in tales of the Vikings in America. Wild grapes do not grow north of the Passamaquoddy Bay, which separates present-day Maine from New Brunswick. Could Leif have wandered as far as Maine or even farther south?

In any event, Leif decided to spend the winter in the spot where he landed and he built a hut large enough to hold his crew of 35 men. They gathered wild berries and grapes, hunted and fished and cut down hardwood trees to fill their hold with the most valued cargo they could take back to Greenland — lumber.

The *Flatey Book* credits another man with having seen the North American continent 14 years before Leif sailed there. He was Bjarni Herjolfsson, a trader who was driven off course to the south while sailing from Iceland to Greenland. Descriptions of the lands he saw indicate that he might have reached Nova Scotia or Newfoundland (which he called Markland) and

Leif Ericsson Lands in the New World

Labrador (which he named Helluland). His crew begged him to go ashore and explore, but Bjarni refused and made his way back to the Greenland settlements.

The next explorer after Leif was his brother, Thorvald, who found Leif's former camp in Vinland and wintered there with 30 men. One day while exploring the coast, they came upon 9 savages hiding under three overturned canoes. They killed 8 of them, but one escaped. The next day the Vikings were attacked by a huge fleet of savages. They fought off the attack, but Thorvald was struck by an arrow — the only man wounded in the battle. Soon afterward he died and was buried on the beach, thus being the first white man killed in America. His companions returned to Greenland.

The tales told about the strange lands to the west stirred the imagination of a remarkable man named Thorfinn Karlsefni. Thorfinn came to Greenland from Iceland in 1002 and married Gudrid, the widow of Eric the Red's son, Thorstein. The next year Thorfinn became the head of an expedition of three ships and 160 men, women and children bound for Vinland. They took cattle with them and intended to form a permanent settlement in the lands to the south and west.

For some reason, probably because of personal jealousy, Leif Ericsson would not give Thorfinn the latitude of Vinland. Without the information Thorfinn did not want to sail directly across the open water from Cape Farewell for fear of missing Vinland entirely. So the expedition sailed north along the Greenland coast to the short crossing in Davis Strait. Then the little ships turned south, crossed Hudson Strait, and continued along the coast of Labrador.

Two days after passing Markland, which they recognized from Bjarni's description, they came to a cape where they found the keel of a wrecked ship. Possibly the spot was present-day Cape Breton and probably the keel was from the ship of some earlier unknown Viking voyager. Thorfinn called the cape Keelness and sailed on south.

Eventually reaching a coast indented with many bays, Thorfinn put his two fastest runners ashore and ordered them to explore to the south. Several days later they returned with wild grapes and wild wheat, and Thorfinn decided to winter in a place nearby which he called the Firth of Currents. His and Gudrid's son Snorri was born there that autumn, the first white child to be born in the New World.

It was an unpleasant winter for the Vikings huddled in tiny huts on a bleak coast. To hunger and cold were added long and heated arguments among the colonists. Why hadn't Thorfinn found the promised Vinland? No one knows today exactly where the Vikings spent that miserable winter.

Viking Raiders' Voyages

Bjarni's First View of America
Karsefni's Expedition to Vinland
Leif Ericsson's Discovery of America

In the spring the chief malcontent, Thorhall, took nine others and one of the ships and sailed north. Apparently he believed they were on an island and wished to round some northern point of land and then sail *south*. But somewhere in his northward voyaging his little ship was struck by a mighty storm and driven east all the way across the Atlantic. Cast up in Ireland, he and his followers were captured and enslaved.

Meanwhile, the others, led by Thorfinn, sailed south "for a long time" to a spot they called Hop. According to the ancient saga, it was at the mouth of a river which flowed into the sea from a lake. Scholars never have agreed on the location of Hop. Some say it was on Mount Hope Bay in Rhode Island. Others argue that it must have been in Nova Scotia. Still another maintains that Thorfinn and his Vikings reached the mouth of the Hudson River.

Whatever the location, the settlers built huts above the lake (which might have been a bay of the ocean). Wild grapes and wheat grew there and the colonists appear to have been content for a time. A couple of weeks after they landed, swarthy, broad-cheeked, large-eyed Indians appeared but were too frightened to come near the strange white people.

It was a more pleasant winter than the previous one. There was plenty of pastureland and the waters abounded with fish, lobsters and other shellfish. Wild ducks and geese swarmed in the marshes while inland

the country was networked by game trails. Throughout the winter they saw no sign of Indians.

One day in the spring, however, the bay suddenly
was dotted with Indians in skin canoes. By signs they
made the Vikings understand they were eager to trade
furs for milk, cheese and red cloth. They came ashore
and all went well until a bull belonging to the Norse
herd — an animal the Indians never had seen — came
charging into their midst. The Indians panicked and
ran in all directions. The Vikings lost their heads too
and attacked the Indians, killing several before the
rest fled.

Now the Vikings dreaded an Indian reprisal raid. It
came presently: a vast horde attacking from all directions. The Vikings recoiled before the attack and two
were killed before the Indians broke off the battle and
withdrew.

Humiliated by their defeat and alarmed by the pros-
pect of continued unequal battle, the Vikings abandoned Hop and returned to the Firth of Currents.
Probably Thorfinn was opposed to quitting Hop but
was outruled by his followers, for he and a few men
returned to Hop for two months before giving it up
forever.

Another winter at the Firth of Currents was passed
amid dissension and heated arguments. In the spring
they loaded their belongings into their two ships and
sailed back to Greenland. As far as is known, it was the

end of Viking attempts to colonize the continent of North America.

Nor is it known whether the Vikings ever penetrated far into the continent from the east coast. Three discoveries of Viking relics inland lead some people to believe that they did. Others discount the relics, however.

In 1898 a farmer near Kensington, Minnesota, uncovered a large flat stone with strange inscriptions while digging a stump from a field. Scholars found a runic inscription on it which they translated: "8 Goths [Swedes] and 22 Norwegians on exploration journey from [or for] Vinland across West. We had camp by two skerries [islands] one day's journey from this stone. We were [?] and fished one day. After we came home found 10 men red with blood and dead. AVM [Ave Maria]. Save from evil. Have 10 men by the sea to look after our ships, 14 days journey from this island. Year 1362."

Some scholars discount this so-called Kensington Stone as not authentic. Others think it might have been carried west from some other place by Indians who believed it held a certain magic.

Another find was a cache of weapons of purported Viking manufacture. The weapons — a broken sword, an ax blade and the metal boss of a shield — were discovered near Lake Nipigon, north of Lake Superior. This so-called Beardsmore Find also has attracted both believers and disbelievers.

Still a third find was an "inscribed stone" which might have been a rune-stone. It came into the possession of Pierre de la Vérendrye, a French explorer who once commanded the trading posts around Lake Nipigon, in the year 1738.

It is true that the Vikings, accustomed to making their way any place a boat would float, could have penetrated the interior of the continent by way of Hudson Bay or the St. Lawrence River and the Great Lakes. But a majority of scholars are skeptical that they actually did, in the light of present evidence.

New evidence was found comparatively recently that Europeans knew about the New World long before Columbus made his historic voyage. In 1957 Yale University scholars found an ancient map folded in an old manuscript which portrayed in faded brownish ink a map of the world done in 1440. It appeared to be a copy of another much earlier map. In addition to a crude representation of Europe, Africa and Asia, it showed Iceland, a surprisingly accurately drawn Greenland, and to the west a coastline labeled "The Island of Vinland, discovered by Bjarni and Leif in Company."

The Viking settlements in Greenland were wiped out and the Vikings' discoveries to the west erased from the memories of Europeans before the 15th Century. So the information drawn on the map of 1440 must have been passed on by word of mouth before it was recorded.

Vinlanda Insula
a Zinurno repa
far leaho fans

← Greenland

Grōdatu

Islanda
Hernia

← LABRADOR

Mare marunum

← NEWFOUNDLAND

Anglia
tena
insula

Rey
franc

Hispanora is.

Muorie
Insula
Beau Bvandum
Brumibie
siere

Desiazair
insula

eux.

Mar: Oceanum

santa insula
Fernina

Portion of map made in 1440 showing Iceland, Greenland and Vinland which is labeled "The Island of Vinland discovered by Bjarni & Leif in Company"

Looking back one thousand years, one can say that the intrepid Vikings were the discoverers of America.

But the word "discovery" implies more than simply going to a place, seeing it, and returning. True discovery, to be accepted by later generations, must be carefully recorded. And a "discovery" should be followed up by other men — as the Spanish followed up the first voyages of Columbus.

As discoverers, the Vikings had two disadvantages. They did not have a recorded language whereby they could communicate their findings and ideas to others. And, as one sees from the ancient sagas, the Vikings lacked weapons superior to those of the enemies they found in the New World.

It has been argued that the Spaniards could not have conquered the New World without gunpowder. It also can be argued that the Vikings could not stay because they lacked it — or some weapon more potent than those of the Indians. Courage brought them to America. But fear for their lives drove them away.

Index

The Author and Artist

WALTER BUEHR, the author and illustrator of numerous books, divides his time between a home in Noroton, Connecticut, an apartment in Manhattan, and a cliff house in the Bahamas. To a book about the Vikings he brings a great deal of foreign travel and intimate knowledge of ships and sailing. He has sailed — among other places — in the Caribbean, the Mediterranean, and the English Channel. Mr. Buehr has designed and built four residences. He began a writing career because he wanted to write a book about ships and the sea which everyone could understand.